VOICES IN PRAISE

A Cappella Creations
for the
Volunteer Choir

TOM FETTKE

illenas PUBLISHING COMPANY

KANSAS CITY, MO 64141

CONTENTS

We Declare Your Majesty

with
Majesty

Words and Music by
MALCOM DU PLESSIS
Arranged by Tom Fettke

Maj - es - ty,_____ wor - ship His maj - es - ty_____
Je - sus who died, now glo - ri - fied, King of all kings.
We de - clare Your maj - es - ty; We pro-
claim that Your name_____ is ex - alt - ed! For You

reign mag - nif - i - cent, You rule vic - to - ri - ous, Your

pow'r is shown thro'-out___ the earth. And we ex -

claim:_____ "Our God is might - y!" Lift up Your

name,_____ for You are ho - ly! Sing it a -

gain, all hon - or and glo - ry! In ad - o -

6

Jesus, What a Wonder You Are

with
Simple Worship

Words and Music by
DAVE BOLTON
Arranged by Tom Fettke

*"Simple Worship"
Warmly ♩= ca. 72

Lord of the worlds be- yond our eyes,

Lord of the end- less star- ry skies,

An- gels all bow to speak Your name.

Here in my heart I do the same.

Let Praises Fill the Sky

To God Be the Glory
Come, Christians, Join to Sing
Sing Hallelujah, Praise the Lord

*"To God Be the Glory"

Arranged by Tom Fettke

Exuberant ♩ = ca. 106

*"Come, Christians, Join to Sing

14

Come as a Child

KEN BIBLE
Inspired by Matthew 11:25-30

TOM FETTKE
Arranged by Tom Fettke

I'm in His Care

Traditional and
TOM FETTKE

Traditional
Arranged by Tom Fettke
and Myra Schubert

care, in His_____ care. King Je-sus got His arms all

care, in His_____ care, I know King

a-round me no e - vil___ tho'ts can a-harm me, For

I thank God, I'm in His_____ care, in His_____

care._____ I thank God, I'm in His_____

care,_____ in His_____ care.

O the Deep, Deep Love of Jesus

SAMUEL TREVOR FRANCIS
and TOM FETTKE

THOMAS WILLIAMS, TOM FETTKE
and CAMP KIRKLAND
Arranged by Tom Fettke

It's About Time

Words and Music by
MERRILL DUNLOP and
PAULINE WILCOX
*Arranged by David Ayers
and Tom Fettke*

Crown Him

with

All Hail the Power of Jesus' Name (DIADEM)

Words and Music by
JEOFF BENWARD
and GALEN BUTLER
Arranged by Tom Fettke

*"All Hail the Power of Jesus' Name"

Majestically ♩ = ca. 126

Instruments of Your Peace

with
Peace

KIRK and DEBY DEARMAN
Based on a prayer by St. Francis of Assisi

KIRK and DEBY DEARMAN
Arranged by Tom Fettke

*"Peace"

p Expressively, with freedom ♩ = ca. 76

Peace,_____ per - fect peace,_____ in this dark world of

sin?_____ The blood of Je - sus whis - pers peace with -

In tempo ♩ = ca. 92

in. Lord, make us in - stru-ments_____ of_____ Your_____

peace; Where there is ha - tred let Your love in -

38

The Lord Is My Strength and My Song

KEN BIBLE
Based on Psalm 118

TOM FETTKE
Arranged by Tom Fettke

I Will Come and Bow Down

Words and Music by
MARTIN NYSTROM
Arranged by Tom Fettke

Sweetly ♩ = ca. 72

Bow down,___ bow down, bow down,___ bow down. bow down. I will come come and bow down at Your feet, Lord Je - sus in Your pres - ence is full - ness of joy.___ There is noth - ing, there is no one who com - pares with You. I take pleas - ure in wor - ship - ing You, Lord.___ I

*If cued divisi is used, omit the highest bass note

Rise!

We Shall Rise (Lister)
Heaven's Jubilee
We Shall Rise (Traditional)

Arranged by Tom Fettke

Until He Comes Again

Words and Music by
JACK HAYFORD
Arranged by Tom Fettke

Declare His Glory

Psalm 96:3-9

JOHN W. PETERSON
Edited by Tom Fettke

With energy ♩ = ca. 108

Lyrics:
De-clare His glo-ry a-mong the hea-then, His won-ders a-mong all peo-ple, For the Lord is great, and great-ly to be praised. He is to be feared a-bove all gods, for the gods of the na-tions are i-dols, but the Lord made the heav-ens— the Lord made the heav-ens. De-clare His

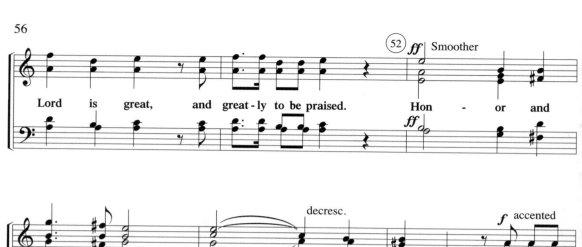

Lord is great, and great-ly to be praised. Hon - or and

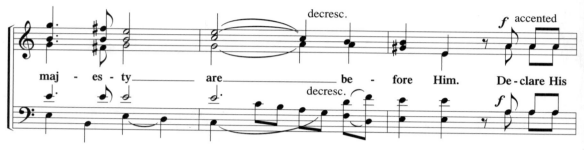

maj - es - ty_____ are_____ be - fore Him. De - clare His

glo - ry a - mong the hea - then, His won - ders a - mong all peo - ple, For the

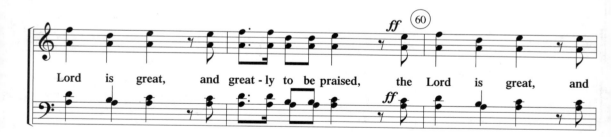

Lord is great, and great - ly to be praised, the Lord is great, and

great - ly to be praised— great - ly to be praised._____

A Quiet Place

with
Near to the Heart of God

Words and Music by
RALPH CARMICHAEL
Arranged by Tom Fettke

*"Near to the Heart of God"

Expressively ♩ = ca. 69

O Je-sus, blest Re-deem-er, Sent from the heart of God, Hold us, who wait be-fore Thee,

Near to the heart of God._____ There is a qui-et place, Far from__ the__ rap-id pace, Where

PLEASE NOTE: Copying of this product is not covered by CCLI licenses. For CCLI information call 1-800-234-2446.

*If cued divisi is used, omit the highest bass note

moun - tain tall, New strength_____ and cour - age there_____ I find. Then from this qui - et place, I go pre - pared to face a man - kind,_____ new day With love for all man - kind, with man - kind,_____ love for all man - kind. man - kind. man - kind.

*If cued divisi is used, omit the highest bass note

The Master Has Come

SARAH DOUDNEY, alt.

TOM FETTKE
Arranged by Tom Fettke

Come Just as You Are

Words and Music by
JOSEPH SABOLICK
Arranged by Tom Fettke

Tenderly ♩ = ca. 72
mp a tempo 2nd time

1,3. Come just as you are;_____ Hear the Spir - it
2. Come just as you are;_____ Hear the Spir - it

mp

Come and see,
Come, re - ceive

call._____ Come just as you are;_____ Come and see
call._____ Come just as you are;_____ Come, re - ceive

come, re - ceive; Come and live_____ for - | ev - er.
Christ, the King; Come and live_____ for - | rit.

come, re - ceive; Come and live for - ev - er._____
Christ, the King; Come and live for -

ev - er - more. *cresc.*
mf

Life ev - er - last - ing, and
stagger breathing
Loo, loo, loo, loo, loo, loo,
mp

ev - er - more._____

cresc.

I Will Trust in the Lord

Traditional Spiritual
and KEN BIBLE

Traditional Spiritual
Arranged by Tom Fettke

(to pg. 66, meas. 1)

2. I will die. 3. I will walk with the

Lord, I will walk with the Lord, I will

walk with the Lord 'til I die. I will

walk with the Lord, I will walk with the Lord, I will

walk with the Lord 'til I die. 4. I will

68

He Giveth More Grace

with
Grace Greater than Our Sin

ANNIE JOHNSON FLINT
"Grace Great than Our Sin"

HUBERT MITCHELL
Arranged by Tom Fettke

With heart ♪ = ca. 96

*If cued divisi is used, omit highest bass note

Victory Chant

Words and Music by
JOSEPH VOGELS
Arranged by Tom Fettke

Per - fect_____ in
Not my will,_____ but

I will praise_____ You all my days. Nah, nah,_____ nah,
want to see_____ Your king - dom come. Nah, nah,_____ nah,

all Your ways.
Yours be done.

nah, nah, nah.
nah, nah, nah.

Per - fect_____ in all Your ways.
Not my will,_____ but

(to pg. 72, meas. 9)

Yours be done. 3. Nah, nah,_____ nah, nah, nah, nah.

3. Glo - ry, glo - ry to the Lamb.

The God of Hope Be with You

KEN BIBLE

TOM FETTKE